Baby Steps in Doomsday Prepping

Also by Gerry LaFemina:

Prose Poems

Notes for the Novice Ventriloquist
Figures from The Big Time Circus Book/The Book of Clown Baby
Zarathustre in Love

Poems

The Story of Ash
Little Heretic
Vanishing Horizon
The Parakeets of Brooklyn
The Window Facing Winter
Graffiti Heart
Voice, Lock, Puppet: Poems of Ali Yuce. Trans/ with Sinan Toprak
Shattered Hours: Poems 1988-1994
23 Below

Fiction

Clamor.
Wish List: Stories

Criticism

Composing Poetry: A Guide to Writing Poems and Thinking Lyrically
Palpable Magic: Essays on Poets and Prosody

Baby Steps in Doomsday Prepping

prose poems

Gerry LaFemina

MADVILLE
PUBLISHING

LAKE DALLAS, TEXAS

FIRST EDITION
Requests for permission to reprint or reuse material from this work should be sent to:

Permissions
Madville Publishing
PO Box 358
Lake Dallas, TX 75065

Acknowledgements:
The author would like to thank the following journals for publishing some of these pieces in somewhat different forms.

Artichoke Haircut	"Is She Really Going Out with Him"
Big City Lit	"Makerel and Bottle"
Blue Lyra Review	"Pocket Watch"
Broadkill Review	"Theory of Special Relativity" and "Utilitarianism—A Love Story"
CDC Poetry Project	"American Poetry"
Cheap Pop	"Thinking of Francis Ponge and You on a Saturday Afternoon"
Coal Hill Review	"Baby Steps in Doomsday Prepping" and "Wing Tips"
Eye to the Telescope	"It's Underneath the Manhole Cover Right Now"
Foundlings	"A Phrenologist Among the Skinheads"
Kestrel	"The Attraction of the Ridiculous," "Gibson Les Paul Double Cutaway," "Landmine," "Modern Times" (as "Chaplin, Modern Times, Lincoln Center, Autumn 2015"), and "One Last Message, One Last Bottle"
Laurel Review	"Last Saturday" and "Uncertainty Principle"
Little Patuxent Review	"A Glass of Water Beside the Bed"
Masque & Spectacle	"Ballet Box," "Ballot Box," "Billet Doux," and "Bullet Box"
Mead	"Tarantula"
Mulberry Fork Review	"Cloudburst" and "Girl Before a Mirror"
Nōd (Calgary)	"Boil"
ReDactions	"After Disaster," "All These Lamps and Yet—" and "My Afternoon with the Critics"
Schuykill Valley Journal	"How I Learned Cruelty" and "Thinking of You"
Sleet Magazine	"Umbrella"
Swamp Ape Review	"Bed" and "Goodwill Diner"
Thin Air	"Last Scene of an Unfilmed Romantic Comedy"
Weave	"A Short Lesson in Human Anatomy"

"Thinking of You" first appeared in *A Cast Iron Aeroplane that Can Actually Fly*, edited by Peter Johnson (2019, Madhat Press).

Cover Design: Jacqueline Davis
Cover Art: "Terminator" by Elena Feliciano
Author Photo: Mercedes Hettich

ISBN: 978-1-948692-24-3 Paper, 978-1-948692-25-0 ebook
Library of Congress Control Number: 2019950603

For Alex

CONTENTS

Baby Steps in Doomsday Prepping

All These Lamps and Yet—

Syllables like flowing water, the house I lived in, close enough to the river to hear it on still nights. It's a still night. That house is fifteen years away. You sleep, mouth open, skin pale against the pale pillow. All the dogs in the building across the street dream of backyards and bones too big to bury, bones stolen, no doubt, from the Museum of Natural History, not so far from here. The characters in the novel I set down wander its sentences, lost without me. I used to sit with a flashlight and a book and a radio. I used to get in trouble. I used to believe in enlightenment, in an age of it coming. I believed, too, in love with a capital L, believed in the upper case abstractions, believed I could list the capitols of Europe where I believed I'd visit. At least I got that last one right. Two blocks away the Hudson says nothing we can distinguish. Every evening now I collect the lower case letters of your name and mine and of the city in which we live, and pour them into a jar. I've punched holes in its lid. I keep it on the bedside table. They glow dimly beside me. Someone dug up Tyrannosaur bones, brought them to New York. Someone filled this apartment with lamps. Beside me you breathe in quiet, convert it to somniloquy, but there's no conversing. Soon the first dogs will stir, but till then it's night still.

CAT AND BIRD

–Paul Klee

The bird is tattooed on the cat's forehead (why wouldn't it be?) and in her disposition to hunt. How she hungers. How she wants. How she stalks the early starlings of February from the window sill, whiskers whisking the pane. Pacing. Pacing. Domesticated jaguar, she won't be distracted, not even by balled-up paper crinkling, crinkling. Not even by a can of tuna turning beneath a blade. Sometimes she crouches as if she could shrink into invisibility, her stillness sudden and necessary. How wicked that I've hung the feeder so near the glass so she might listen to the chirping chirping, and later to the angry chatter of jays who taunt Tesla, exposing a white breast to her as if to say, *white meat, right here*, wings outspread, daring. How serious is she in her desire and frustration. How like any of us when looking longing in the eye.

TAXIDERMY/JIGSAW

Because she was articulate with her ardor, brought with affection gifts she left beside the bed, my cat will have a tenth life, not as a name engraved on a mahogany box of grit and minerals on the mantel, nor buried beneath a small mound behind the back garden as if she'd been a spaniel named Sparky. And no, I won't do what a former landlord did with his dead Irish Setter, stuffed, forever sitting, one paw up as if to shake. Instead, let's have the taxidermist remove the flesh and viscera from the bones, strip the muscles, too, until she's nothing but puzzle pieces, re-articulated, a feline skeleton back from the prowl, all femur and rib cage like she never was, the small skeleton of a vole trapped in her jaw, its thin spine asplinter, cat teeth almost grinning, so proud of herself. Now, when I miss her, I might gaze at the skull, pet each vertebrae with my index finger, saying again, what a good girl she is.

SCHROEDINGER'S BOX

Forget the cat. The box (not a cat box but a box fit for a cat) is what's important. How magical it must be that we can't know what's inside, whether what we left there remains. More like mother's pocketbook—how things vanished within till they were found again—money, Lifesavers, what have you. Is it cardboard, plastic, wooden with brass hinges and a small latch? Science doesn't specify, but all of physics must be inside, like the Arc of the Covenant, like a safe for the Hope Diamond, like the ring box for the engagement never engaged. Does the love still exist? What is that hurt, that yowling?

Hive Mind

There's a bee in the classroom, not a particularly large one, smaller than my small toe. It wears a black and yellow striped sweater, translucent wings.

There's a bee in the classroom, and my college students point and duck their heads. They forget they are seventeen Godzillas to the bee. None of them are allergic, so I'm bemused by their sudden, startled shrieks.

We've been talking about the muse up until this point, today—how I don't believe in such a thing. This stings their sensibilities. The bee in the classroom is a happy distraction. Their reactions prevent them from seeing the possible poems in the way its antennae move.

There's a bee in the classroom. My students are all abuzz. I mention the fuzzy socks it wears. They're confused I find it cute. They ask me to kill it—it's only a bee, after all, a worker. And my karma,

There's a bee in the classroom. I want to keep it in an apiary of one, make it the class mascot for the bee brings gold. Maybe there's an NEA or Guggenheim or MacArthur genius among us. I suggest after class they all go for mead. Suggest no one's at risk if they're not pollen-full, blossoming, but they don't listen because

there's a bee in the classroom. Exasperated I open the window, finally, until it flees, flying free into early autumn. My students swarm to watch from their new found safety. I can see the children they were only twelve years ago. One girl waves to it, that small thing growing smaller in the afternoon's honeyed light.

Goodwill Diner

The cheapest joint in town, with the new-to-you foods the foodies keep jonesing about, just a smorgasbord of yesterday's half-eaten burgers, Mongolian pork over rice, chicken kabob with couscous. Almost any cuisine could be the plat du jour. You want the dark-meat turkey and mashed potatoes? How about spaghetti? Low overhead is the secret. No keeping up with the Joneses. No one ever sends a plate back though sometimes a customer complains the portions are too small. Remember, you have to get there early—with every order the waitstaff scratches another dish off the menu.

BILLET DOUX

Cara mia, I left the sweets for you, those caramels, kisses, non-pareils. The chocolate rich and smooth as skin. I brought, too, the doves of my devotion. They coo carefree in their rooftop coop unaware of the peregrine falcon circling above. There's more to come, so forgive, sweetheart, these sweet notes with their crosshair Xs, their bullet hole Os, straight from the midway shooting range. I know they must bedevil you, riddled as they are with the riddle that is *amore*.

THE ATTRACTION OF THE RIDICULOUS

Since it's hard to be serious about people so serious, talk to me instead about the sublimity of buffoons. I know, some like their men buff, their women busty, hair-dos just so (page boys, beehives, bouffants, what have you), smiles white and orderly as china. And yes, some so-and-sos prefer the dramatic or melodramatic types (though I've always thought a dram of drama is damn near enough, thank you). Others want the silent kind, about which there is nothing to say. Freaks aren't sexy, yet they do have their appeal. No. No. Just make me laugh. Get me to bust a gut. Crack me up in the car and in the kitchen and in the supermarket among the dull-faced cans of crushed tomatoes and the doll-faced cart pushers, stupified and blinking.

INCONVENIENCE STORE

Its hours aren't posted, and even if they were, the sign would just say *best guess*. Its website doesn't exist, and you enter around back as the front doors are stuck, the sign above says the wrong name. Everything you want is in the storeroom or on a shelf too high to reach. You try your tip toes. You try a milk crate. You stretch. You ask another shopper. Nothing works. There's not a clerk or stockboy to be seen. One thousand cans of octopus, stacked in a pyramid that would make a pharaoh proud, all out of date. The cashiers close their registers before you get to their lines with your cartful of missed opportunities. You have to have exact change; the only credit card they take is Prussian Express. They don't take returns, not even for store credit. It's such a hassle, but it's the nearest shop for miles.

Elementary

For my tenth Christmas I wanted a Mongoose bicycle, and today a boy is sentenced in juvenile court for attempting to murder his favorite cheerleader. The sun through the leaves casts its vicious green light on all of us, even my mother who reads Sherlock Holmes so she can meet in Victorian dress with the Sherlockians come December. I wanted that bike so I could deliver newspapers after school, throwing them at front doors all over Staten Island, then across the Verrazano Bridge into Brooklyn, Queens . . . Of course, I knew I couldn't really, just as I knew Wile E. Coyote couldn't survive the fall from those cliffs into the barren canyons below. I was a misfit on the ball field and at the kitchen table, both. Sister Marcella used to say: *Don't sit like a brick at your desk*. I wanted to be a brick through the rear window of a car. I served a lunch of honeysuckle and sunlight to my first girlfriend then. We ate, gluttonous. This never happened. I gave her my crayon Valentine, and thus walked the schoolyard with the empty belly of broken-heartedness. I wanted to gift wrap all my petty grievances and slide them under the tree with a tag that said *to all you motherfuckers*. I wanted that bicycle, wanted to pedal fast and far from it all. Instead I got a model of the Millenium Falcon, which I knew would never hit hyperspace, never even escape the gravity of that neighborhood.

Is She Really Going Out with Him

–Joe Jackson

Was I only 13 then? Lined up with classmates in the playground waiting for the mad dash toward high school and planning our graduation dance, I had nothing but some broken home fragments that rattled like latchkeys in my pockets—how I scratched my fingers on them from time to time. There were girls I dreamt about; surely their eighth grade boyfriends I believed were never good enough because they weren't me. Joe Jackson on the Top 40 those weeks—Casey Kasem moving him closer to the chart top each Saturday, counting down. It wasn't disco. It wasn't the blues, though I wanted to use the gravel I consumed each hour to growl along and shimmy my hips. I dreamt dance floors, dreamt of Eileen, of Suzette, of Jill, dreamt so many faces I can't even name. The world was changing, our bodies were changing, my music, too. In another year I'd howl along with buzz saw guitars & tommy gun drums as if my bones could no longer bear frustration.

Is she really gonna take him home tonight?

Joe knew the answer. Only 13, I did, too: *duh*. Thus we learned the order of things, and thus we stepped closer to becoming the adults we never foresaw as in a dark room a radio played the national anthem of the small country that is the self.

Rocket Lanes

Hundreds—no, thousands—of multi-colored shoes. A display case of trophies like the ones my brother had in his basement room: *Perfect Game, League Best* . . . Smell of French fry grease from the snack bar. Pin thunder and sometimes a collective, frustrated groan or else the lone *shit* of some guy on lane 15. Who hasn't been the lone guy on lane 15? Once, there'd been pin boys and soda jerks, now it's just one woman dishing out scorecards and making change. She keeps a paperback novel by the cash register. Sometimes there are birthday parties. Ten spots change hands: another loser, another winner. Sometimes the too-serious league bowlers rush us from our games because their frames are more important. So many early dates there, and this one just another of them, how she claps with each strike, each spare. There's a history of gutter tosses, handicaps, and one-pin losses that could be the diary I didn't keep. When her ex shows up, no one's surprised by the threat of violence. Somewhere a boomer hooks into the pocket with an explosion of pins. On the racks along the back walls, the balls—most black, but some speckled reds, oranges, blues—all of them waxed and gleaming as if, if we looked intently enough, we could see a future in them.

THEORY OF SPECIAL RELATIVITY

The grandfather clock towers above the watches, as if reading them a story. It begins *Once upon a time . . .* The watch faces seem alive, the way light glints off their glass, their small hands outstretched. Everything has come to a standstill but the light through the window and the dust. There is nothing to be alarmed about. This story has history; it's been told for generations.

Outside people hurry past. Church bells count the quarters, one of the few reminders of another era, back when miners sat at the local diner after clocking out.

You know the spiel, no on can predict this future, and the past is dismantled daily. Time was there used to be a glockenspiel in the town square. At noon and six the bells would chime, and from the clock a young master and miss would go through their pantomime. They'd meet in the middle. He'd bow, she'd bow, then they'd kiss.

It didn't matter how many times they'd seen this little show, people still would stop. Watch.

A Room for Space Agers

A disciple of *The Jetsons*, I dreamt myself James T. Kirk (Oh, to be loved by a green-skinned alien in a bikini, to fire a phaser on stun). Constellations pasted to the ceiling above my bed provided the only warmth when the lights were out. I first walked the day men walked on the moon (one small step for me in a Brooklyn living room, one giant leap . . .). I biked to the store, saved my pennies for the inevitable jetpack, and learned to run for the bomb shelter, to hide myself under a desk. Sonic booms and mushroom clouds were the metaphor for my parents' divorce, the merit badges of my Boy Scout troop. Flying saucers might've visited, but never arrived. I kept a telescope by my window to watch for them. The model rocketships I never learned to launch, the countdown to blast off always aborted. At a certain age I re-aimed that telescope, first, to look into the window of the young widow across the street, she who made me feel atomic. Then a few weeks later I turned the 'scope around so I might look out onto a world so small I could fit it all in my fist.

THE COMET

It is a locket dragging its chain across the horizon. Imagine, someone took it off, flung it, angry and hurt. It hurries across the sky then it's gone for another fifty-some years, almost forgotten till some guys calls your name in a bar called The Observatory. But it's not you. It's not even someone who looks like you. It's just the single syllable of your first name trailed by laughter over glass bottles. The comet reaches the outer limits of its orbit and returns. Outside, clouds obscure everything, even the cracked door of light the moon casts. Even the stars like scattered earrings, gone.

Shore Thing

Blue sky with clouds and sunlight. Gravity kept me and everything else grounded except the gulls. These are the things I'm sure of. Waves struck the strand though I couldn't say whether the tide was high or low. Most likely, shifting. Beach grasses—knee high and thin, whittled sharp—swayed with whatever way the wind sashayed. Ships bobbed at the horizon, so far away they seemed left behind by a child. Closer to shore, the swim buoys provided a perch for a few royal terns. No one swam, though some sat on distant porches in the shade. Your footprints trailed behind you between breakers and the wrack line as did mine. Almost parallel. Almost. Not that it matters because a boy comes everyday with a rake to smooth the sand, to erase all trace of what had been.

COLLECTION

In my life I've gathered maybe five perfect rocks. It isn't that they were smooth or handsomely speckled with rare minerals. No, they were often misshapen, pitted, easily forgettable. The first I'd kicked the entire way home from school when I was a child. In my pocket it became a charm, the imagined shatterer of plate glass, ammunition for the slingshot I never owned. Another was yellow and spotted like a cheetah. I cut my finger on the third's sharp edge; it seemed to absorb my blood in its iron tint. The fourth was a the pebble I kept beneath my tongue so I wouldn't succumb to the temptation to kiss just anyone. I found the fifth stone at the shore, marbleized, the size of my fist, the shape not of a valentine but of an animal heart, and seemingly chambered. I kept it in the car with me for a long time until the woman I slept beside asked why I kept it. What could I say about the geology of ardor? Only how heavy the chest is, how even now, when I swim far from shore there's the risk of going under, to settle into the sand, into the mineral earth, the water nothing but brilliant ripples, buoy bells tolling.

Gibson Les Paul Double Cutaway

For its six strings exist, one for each finger of the fretting hand and one more to confuse the novice.

For although it's made for our feral souls to rock, to scream, to shred, unplugged it weeps gently in my arms like a lover once did, a few days before she decided it was all over.

For it knows harmony and harmonics, major chords and discord, the feel of my fingers firm, tips calloused, on its neck.

For it reflects light and absorbs light simultaneously, like a sunbather. How I want and don't want to turn away. Thus the guitar teaches us again ambivalence.

For plugged in it squeals like locomotive chug-chug-chugging through the bad side of town, the crossings down, clanging. We call this tone.

For I have looked on, jealous, when it's in the grip of another. How she coaxed it to sing with her touch. Her expression was, I imagine, that of angels when God made the heaven and the earth and declared it was good.

For the struck power chord and sustain like a mini big bang because music was and wasn't at the creation.

For its double cutaway gives it the look of devil's horns. This is why kids stretch out pinky and index finger from their hands, arms rocking to the beat.

For rock-n-roll, preacher said, is Lucifer's music, so I wrote for weeks a song called "Paradise Regained," all pentatonic and palm mute.

For at the end of the night I rest it in its cradle, and still I'm just a punk who knows little but down stroke, treble, and trouble.

For it is the bad side of town.

For I've repented and trespassed again, head banging. All barre chord and boogie. All feedback and growl. All torch song and dirge.

Concert Chamber

– Unknown

Of course, the concert could be over, but more likely, it's still waiting to occur: sheets unfolded, notes eager for the eyes of the players, and the guitar at attention on its stand, waiting to be held again, to be touched in the way all musicians love their instruments: the violin nuzzled against the fiddler's chin, the mouthpiece kissed by the brass section's first trumpet. Candles have been lit to set the mood.

What of the classical guitarists I knew in school, whom I didn't jive with, the way they would coat their fingernails in layers of crazy glue, strengthening them for the pluck and strum. Those days, I was addicted to wattage and volume, to the vibrations of my addled heart. 110 volts. 16 ohms. Speakers stacked on stage, like a magician's cabinet where the girl might enter, disappear. That's a different story.

In my morning living room I crave today silence, snow falling out the window white in the predawn dark. Soon, the first car starting like a conductor clearing his throat.

Bullet Box

By nine we'd be on our rounds with an empty carton to collect the casings. They glowed brassy and bad ass in the alleys mornings-after, the rounds discharged. We didn't like to think why or who at. In case you forgot: they'd billeted a militia a few blocks from here. In case you forgot: some live; some die. These are the ground rules we wake up to. Nights I'd stare at the ceiling listening to .45 thunder, cower under the sheets like it were a special Saturday night. When the bull of my pulse stampeded, keeping me from sleep for hours, I'd hold one of those shells to my ear hoping to hear the ocean's lullaby.

One Last Message, One Last Bottle

No one would confuse me with J. Alfred. No one would confuse me with Robinson C. There's no Friday here, and no other days of the week either. If you don't know what too much sun and isolation can do, so be it. Let me just say, there's only so much fish and cocoanuts a man can stand, therefore I'm penciling in scurvy for the next full moon. Yesterday I heard music, the voice viciously beautiful, and all I could think was *company!* Whether you believe me or not, I didn't want it to be a mermaid song that high-pitched melody, mellifluous above the beat of the surf. Last month was the end of monsoon season, and the days had become a monotony of white sands and whitecaps. Despite that description, this is no paradise even with lobster regularly on the menu. I heard singing and I wanted it to be you, but those melodies resonating from the shore were nothing more than trade winds kissing the mouths of bottles. Such a miserable calypso when I realized the notes inside them were the very ones I'd addressed to you the year before.

Thinking of Francis Ponge and You on a Saturday Afternoon

A man creates giant soap bubbles in the park. He has a sudsy bucket, a wand of butcher string and bamboo rods, a way of waving his arms like a conjurer. His bubbles are larger than basketballs, loom like hansome cabs with happy couples in the back. The bubbles float, sunlight shimmering in the spectrum along their flanks.

Soon he invites children to join him. Smaller bubbles appear. Some blow up in soft explosions of suds. Others, little dirigibles, ascend nearer the tree branches and shimmy in the slight breeze. Delicate and short lived, they wobble, uncertain in their beauty. I want to reach out and touch one the way I wish to trace a finger along your cheek.

I'd tell you right now how I love you but fear the moment bursting, fear getting my mouth washed out with soap.

Utilitarianism —A Love Story

When she called me a cad, there was little I could argue. I'd come to learn by then (as most men do) to agree for she was usually right. When called a rake, though, I understood a simple truth and knew what I might do. I went out, got red and golden maple leaves tattooed around my ankles and feet, a few twigs stuck among them for good measure. *See*, I said, my voice cool as November, *I'm no longer so useless.* That night she hung me up on the peg board in the garage. Sure, I was a tool, but she knew how to handle me.

Umbrella

In this gale, the giant bat of my umbrella flaps furiously. Like an old hurt, it risks tugging me away, the way it overwhelms—how suddenly I dangle from a hook seven stories above the city. All my super hero fantasies proven wrong: I can't save even myself. The girl stopped on her bicycle, pointing at me, isn't amazed or excited but terrified. I'm careening between lampposts and billboards; birds squawk, frightened; then another gust sets me spiraling even higher. Below, nothing but concrete, asphalt, impact. Above, cloud cover lowers its furrowed brow and erupts with lightning. Why shouldn't I let go to gravity?

Monkeywrench

Not the lemur wrench or the gorilla wrench, no, nothing as new-fangled, as open to possibility as those, but an old fashioned monkeywrench, thick-handled, thick-headed, clumsy but remaining all-purpose.

Despite the rumors there was no Mister Moncky, for whom the wrench is named. We'd call him a mensch for creating such a utilitarian tool. Nor is it known for being so versatile that even a monkey could use it. There's a monkey mystery, a monkeywrench thrown into etymology.

My mother was a firm believer in the crescent wrench, which she referred to as a monkeywrench, with which it shares an important characteristic: an adjustable head.

If I could, I'd present a graphic. Suffice to say it has a handle, an adjustor, and adjustable jaws with a pair of grips.

All day, I've been building the machine with spare scraps from the work bench: different nuts, different bolts. So many head sizes: metrics and ASE. So many hours of labor. So many cogs and sprockets set. Tightening, loosening, and still so much remains undone.

It's Under the Manhole Cover Right Now

—overheard on First Ave.
—for LL

It's breathing fire. It's smoking cigarettes or hashish. It's got asthma, a cell phone, and your number. It's a small disaster—a party of your exes talking about you. To your mother. No, to my mother. A party of my exes talking about you. Someone's decided on orange cones and hard hats. Someone's decided to divert traffic, to consult charts. The problem's being worked on right now, they assure. It's not from another planet, another country, another town. We're not talking terrorism. There's no need for sirens, no need for the nightly news. It's a minor emergency but a real one, like missing you.

Boil

There's an abscess in my chest right below my right nipple, the very place where she used to rest her head, those overheated nights after the sweat-making, the calling to angels and each other, after the saliva and cum, after the room returned to focus, a porch light from across the street beckoning. Imagine all the sweet-somethings I whispered into her left ear leaked out, spilled across my chest, the sponge of my flesh soaking them up. And all the lies, too. And all the hopes we'd held on to from before we'd ever met. How they festered and grew with pus. Some days I think to lance it, let it drain, squeezing it to make sure the last of the infection's gone. Mostly I just touch it with the tip of my finger, with an aching kind of longing, the way I'd touch the swell of her labia, and sigh the name of the beloved nobody in my room.

Modern Times

–Charlie Chaplin
–Lincoln Center, Autumn 2015

A late birthday present, even the way you adjust my tie. Like many silent films, it's a love story, just listen to the orchestra playing the soundtrack: "Smile" cascading toward crescendo. And you, beautiful in a gown that touched you like I would touch you. Because these are post-modern times, nothing, not even romance, is so simple, not even the violin at the musician's chin, not even applause and laughter, not even the way you will lean into me when we walk back to our door. Shipbuilder's apprentice, factory hand, night watchman—what wouldn't he do for her? It's late September, so much ending we couldn't foresee. At movie's end the Tramp and the Gamin (Chaplin and Goddard) walk an empty road toward whatever future is beyond the last chord's waning. Like wanting you, the traffic on Broadway relentless as it passes.

Thinking of Charles Bronson

Not the action actor but a guy I met at the Library. Not a library, but the bar on Avenue A that serves cheap whiskey, the place with books spilled on tables or else face down, drunk on shelves too dimly lit to see.

He told everyone his parents named him Charles, so he might grow tough and steel-tongued. It helped, of course, that he already possessed that surname though he could've been called Clint Eastwood Bronson or John Wayne Bronson, the way a cheeseburger might be dubbed El Burger Supremo on a menu just to get us to think differently about ground sirloin, cheese, ketchup; the way being called *honey* by a lover remakes us, transforms how we look next time we glance at the mirror.

Someone played "99 Red Balloons" on the jukebox, someone ordered a cheeseburger and swore it was delicious. I asked for another bourbon. *Sweetheart*, the bar girl said, *I think you've had enough.* I stumbled out the door, intoxicated on I don't know what, bumbled right past Bronson who was fumbling through a table of contents. He was looking thoughtful like he might kill somebody. Looking like he might cry.

Baby Steps in Doomsday Prepping

I have three jugs of water, some canned goods, a propane stove. I have a shovel, blueprints, and big enough back yard. I still don't own a pistol. Because I've seen the *Twilight Zone*, I've several spare pairs of glasses. Because I may have to repopulate the planet, I might start looking for a mate. Maybe I'll ask someone out on a date. How's that for a pick-up line? Maybe not tonight. I should buy some survivalist literature, maybe a how-to book. I should get a can opener, a pocketknife, another propane tank, another fedora. I could make a checklist. I shouldn't procrastinate. Some scholars think it took Noah 120 years to construct the ark; others have recalculated, say it was half that. Tomorrow maybe I'll buy cement blocks and concrete. The cupcakes I bought won't last till the apocalypse, but that's okay: I have plenty of time, and they are so tasty.

After Disaster

In a hangar the investigators are at work, rebuilding the jet from recovered debris. They have the black box. The cockpit voice recorder. There's a team of them. Some fragments are no bigger than my hand or my heart; some of the pieces are obvious, others could be many things. The work isn't done in quiet: conversation and opinions and arguments are the norm. The plane went down in a storm. There's plenty of speculation. The co-pilot's last words were *I can't do this anymore.* Some sentences can't be deciphered. They're trying to figure out what happened so they might avoid another catastrophe. They're like any of us. They've been at it for months but can work no faster. Even today, fresh findings from the debris field arrive. It's so strange—isn't it?—the way it makes their voices rise with excitement and expectations.

Tangiers

To see the sunlight on its white buildings and glass is to glance into the teary eye of God himself and to risk madness in the saline air. Salvation may be sought in its bazaars, where men in fezzes drink thick coffee while veiled women in shawls sell trinkets and talismans for luck. Here, they still talk of the Cave of Hercules, just beyond the city gates. Here, they give directions with their hands, zig-zagging you through alleys and stalls where you will find the ordinary (cell phones, spices, lapis lazuli) and the bizarre (golden scarab from ancient crypts, petrified camel eyes).

In the heat a tongue will thicken with want for kisses. Water tastes bitterly delicious in Tangiers. The night sky reveals itself as an indigo tapestry unfurled and bejeweled. The music in the cafes and clubs throbs, hypnotic like the hips of a young woman who dances, who lures you with one curled fingers.

Love is like Tangiers, or is it the other way around? Exotic. Unforgettable. The salt air of Gibraltar blows cool. I only visited once, years ago and learned the unbearable truths about beauty. I vowed I'd never go back.

A Glass of Water Beside the Bed

This oasis in the desert of night is no mirage. It collects what little light burns through the window and holds it in its cupped palms like the moon snared in a swimming pool.

I've wandered miles across the sheets. When I wake beside her, I tip back the glass as if to cleanse myself on what might be the holiest day of the year.

Outside, a sudden rain founds its church of puddles on the sidewalks, and nightcrawlers rise from soil as they do, fodder for the flock in the low branches.

Uncertainty Principle

I'm sure I will see you at the other side of sleep—not in my dreams (though who knows, I rarely recall them and there was that one . . .), but in the morning or some time after lunch, certainly by supper. I will see you after the movie ends, I'm sure, in the lobby, both of us blinking in the popcorn and Coca-Cola light. I will see you if you don't see me first. I will, I'm sure, see you at Columbus Circle where we've met before in winter with Captain Christopher as witness. The new world forever waiting, always fresh. I will see you at 3:00 though we said 2:30 for you are usually late. I'm sure. I'm sure I will see you after the dance, your partner exhausted, mine a closeted gown of excuses—we will drink white wine, the goblets open mouthed with laughter. I will see you after Christmas, at the end of the sky ride that has been this year: I'll be seated on the bench of New Year's Day, your face flushed from a midnight kiss, mine blushed with too much bourbon and desire. Always desire. I'm sure I will see you after the bus trip, after the sobbing, after the long insomniac night. I will see you after fire and after frost. After church. On the other side of the platform. On the other side of the bed, no. On the other side of the country, perhaps—I will see you (shall we plan on it?) in Santa Barbara, Santa Monica, Santa Cruz. I will see you, I'm sure, seated not with the saints, not with the sinners: you will be an iconoclast among icons. I'm sure I will see you on the other side of a table set for two, dressed unprovocatively seductive, a haiku of acne on your cheek but that's the future and right now, when even the subways have gone to Z's, and even the night watchman aboard a docked replica of the Santa Maria, stretches and dozes off to see whomever he dreams about, right now I'm almost positive I will see you some time tomorrow, or at least, at the very least, I am sure, by the end of the week.

American Poetry

In Memory of Thomas Lux

I recognize these claims I make are not science-based. I praise American poetry's diversity for its diversity is its strength. Each poem conceived in a climax of inspiration— an image or an overheard phrase, or a word banned by bureaucrats, committees or point-totaling politicians, or you name it. Then the gestation of drafts.

I'm aware this is a terrible metaphor, but the poem becomes fetus and eventually gets its entitlement of a title. Most Americans don't care, don't read poems any more than they read medical journals. They remain ambivalent about peer reviews. Not that it matters.

Nor does it matter that sometimes revisions are transgenre-d—prose poems longing for lineation and vice versa: verse (free and formal both) believing it should be a paragraph, wanting only the cadence of the sentence. How vulnerable each word, each syllable. What evidence-based claims might the critics down the hall make with their deconstructions about these matters? I couldn't construct their hypotheses or their outcomes, only know the myths of their methodologies. I wouldn't want anything else. I recognize my claims are not science-based, but I praise American poetry for its diversity. Its diversity is its strength.

Still Life with Dead Game

—Willem van Aelst

Forget the rabbit and rooster of the painting, for in the scene I'm reminded of, a deer hangs by its hind ankles, antlers almost touching the pool of blood seeping beneath the buck pole. The three dead squirrels used for target practice in the early morning just because and kept with the deer for the same reason—not, certainly for the quality of the meat, though we were poor and the looming winter long and bitter as some marriages in Northern Michigan. Already the third snow had fallen, which is why the red is so brilliant, and why, too, the face of the deer is nearly reflected in it. Thanksgiving still eight days away, hence, later, the butchering, the harder work of preparing this for the larder. It's hard, I know, not to look away, but the meat is our meat, so with gratitude we pray.

The Squirrels of Houghton Lake

They are born of the trees but quickly learn they aren't avian although, for sure, they've learned bird language. They speak it with an accent and have some specialized chirps only they know.

In their furry black leotards they are a sight—the whole troupe of them. In the right light they look silky; in other light they look furious.

They leap from tree limb to bird feeder, roof edge to bird feeder, bird feeder to trellis. They disdain passers by, many of whom seem ready to applaud. Children like to point, *ooh* and *ahh*.

The jays, however, don't appreciate them. They squawk *Thief!* in their throaty way, but the squirrels pay no mind as it sounds so much like *Encore! Encore!*

Personally, I love to watch one in the early light as it pops the top of an acorn. Like a wino with an open bottle, it looks both ways, chirps with happiness, and brings it to its mouth.

Ballot Box

The only time I ran for office the returns were delivered by our civics teacher. Since my nomination my campaign had been phenomenal, and if casinos gave odds for high school elections, Bally's would have had me at 2:1. But this was the Balkans of suburbia. The bullies had done their jobs: there'd been threats, posters ripped from the bulletin boards, talk in the detention hall. No inspectors watched the polls. When the bell closed down the class day, our instructor read the results. No surprise I lost, but with negative numbers? The three classmates who penciled in *Anyone but G–*, I can surmise. Thus I went down in history. I confess my concession speech was written under duress, for even my friends had defected as we'd all been reminded they'd built the internment camp of the coat closet close by.

How I Learned Cruelty

I made a model snowman out of three scoops of vanilla ice cream, some chocolate sprinkles for eyes and a nose.

Then I let him melt, there in the bowl, the slow metamorphosis of solid to liquid, his features uglifying, getting less defined, till he fell over, a white puddle growing.

My spoon in the dish like the grave digger's shovel.

Pencil

Little harpoon I spear into the sea of this page, this ocean of possibility. The whale's blood rises to the surface as words, the most abridged edition of *Moby Dick*.

Frisbee

It's hard not to love the word, the way it stretches from the mouth, its extended ēē streaming into the open air like the thing itself, swirling through the evening sky.

Frisbee football. Frisbee golf. A game of catch. Another of fetch. How simple it seems, now that we all have forgotten how easily it hooked away from our target.

Who was I tossing it to? Not the girls in the commercial—Wham-O—who always seemed to smile at their boyfriends. Remember how effortlessly those guys caught it behind their backs or else by tapping it first from underneath so it paused in place and spun like a galaxy.

And that glow-in-the-dark one we owned in a different decade, in the decadent century, when we were readily awed by phosphors? It appeared to hover when flung right, greenish-white in the dusk, alight from within: a flying saucer of tiny Gullivers to visit Brobdingnarian earth. Fading, still it startled, florescent, when I'd wake late night from dream picnics, those dates I didn't go on, those girls whose names I loved on my tongue, in my mouth, in 2 A.M.'s dismal solitude.

No one in those ads had hair that frizzed. Not once did a disc hit a hive of bees, send everyone shrieking. The whole world had been airbrushed into perfection. Oh, that radiant toy, it wasn't a UFO though it was the future, and it seemed like the invasion had finally come.

Towel

Tossed aside the way it is, it could be a discarded map to an unknown country, and aren't we the immigrant type—curious, hungry, meek, entrepreneurial.

Don't confuse it with the cloth Veronica used to wipe Christ's face, only to find his features sustained in the fabric. No, this towel's a bit soiled, perhaps, but plain and white, almost dull.

It's been the dress-down dress, the sarong, the toga, the kilt.

Damp and left on the floor, with its scent of you: the dropped flag of surrender, of that tiny kingdom we call home.

Bed

Pickup truck to the kingdom of dreams, I've been its cargo for decades, smuggled beneath blankets, without papers. Nights I struggled to sleep, the road there potholed, the driver steering sharply to and fro. I turned and tossed with the restlessness of a refugee. And some nights I woke accosted by darkness, thinking we were lost; what I thought was the North Star just a lit window across the street, maybe a neighbor tending her crying baby, while you stirred beside me, muttering softly in the forgotten language of that foreign land.

Soviet Kitchenette

I lived in Little Kiev (formerly Dinky Krakow) in my Polish Aunt's apartment long after Glasnost. The voices of bloc refugees guttural in the elevators. Scent of *syrniki* and *kruchenyky* heavy in the sea foam hallways.

The Russians, rumor has it, live in Coney Island on blocks dubbed Mini Moscow and Petite Petersburg. They feed the black pigeons crumbs from black bread in a meager Red Square. They say the *borscht* there is to die for.

When the Cuban restaurant we went to closed, when the Uzbeki diner lowered its grate for the last time like a curtain being drawn, I stayed stoic. Now Odessa, that lousy dive of midnight pirogi and blintzes, is locking its doors, too, my favorite waitresses banished to the Siberia of unemployment; myself, to the gulag of loneliness.

Having escaped the Cossacks, my aunt wouldn't tolerate my disappointment. There in that cramped galley she'd prepare the kielbasa and cabbage and goulash. She wasn't the best cook, like her vain sister was, but she did understand our starkest comforts.

BEFORE THE BANQUET

—Caleb

There's the table and chairs. The kitchen. The market. Here's the guest list and the not-on-your-life-will-you-invite-them list. Now comes the caterers and trays of *hors d'oeuvres*.

Remember: this is only a test run. You need to envision who sits beside whom, who sits across from whom, who must sit on the far side of the room. Imagine the conversations and where the first disagreement might rise like an emergency flare. Plan for the unforeseen. You have to script the toast. You have to taste the roast. Disinvite the gluten-free people. The vegans. The Atkins dieters. The Joneses. Order more bottles of wine. Raise your glass and praise its fruity bouquet. Do it all again in a few days. Revise the menu. The banquet remains a few weeks away.

A Phrenologist Among Skinheads

Some of these punters have heads cratered like moons, their skulls bumped and battered by fisticuffs and accidents. That one like he'd been dropped feet-last as a toddler. Still some have had their skulls buffed as if for a photo shoot. Even the women with their frill of bangs like valances look as though they've been hanging out in low ceilinged places and standing too quickly.

These heads, like epic poems to be read by fingertip. They've made it so easy to study our propensities, faculties and sentiments. Even the smoothest one, with skin stretched satiny along the clean curve of its dome, not even a razor cut, not even stubble, think about it: what a story it might tell.

My Afternoon with the Critics

I rode with Foucault in his Renault Reliant to watch porno with Adorno on a torn couch beside the icon of Lacan. Derrida was there, as well, and he deconstructed every derriere and erection until Linda Hutchinson leaned in noting the graphic historiographic fiction of the friction. *Fuck it*, I thought, and left to play Atari with Guattari but rarely with Deleuze against whom I usually lose.

How

Pay no heed to the best minds of my generation, pay no heed at all, for these aren't them, these Gen X refugees opening the garage door to middle age; they wonder and worry about pension plans and portfolio performance, their flunking children, their flunky jobs, their parents on cruises in the retirement seas, dancing to funk and soul they themselves refuse to enjoy; how sad they no longer fit into old leather jackets, into hip record stores, into those worn slacker slacks they always wore, thus they sit at the bar, heads tilted, listening to song after song on the juke box, waiting for Nirvana, unsure how it came to this.

Ballet Box

Not a waltz. Not a tango or merengue. Not a macarena or hustle or even a belly dance. Not a billion of the mass produced, but maybe a million. Wind it up and the dancer dances, arms above head, feet on point, she twirls to the disjointed melody of sugar plum fairies. The young girl sleeps beneath toe shoes. She dreams of gypsies in position one and then batterie. She winds the key when Mother says *bed time* and then slips between blankets into dreams of tutus and tights. Such a simple but brilliant gift: like her dreams, it requires no batteries. She just winds the key (*not too far*, Mother says when she says good night, *we don't want it to break*) and the dancer dances, twirls until the song ends and then goes limp.

Last Scene of an Unfilmed Romantic Comedy

We've been rooting for them, of course, such is the nature of the genre. He's been in the Merchant Marines for the last three years, hoping the seas would seize the memory of her. They haven't. She's now in the Mermaid Parade, back in the Coney Island of her childhood. He used to be the guy who served her lemon ices, the white scoops like her breasts then, pale lace of sweat across them on the hottest days.

All that's in flashback and from early in the script when we're getting to know them— so many missed connections, the unsaid sentences. No one would call her Calypso despite every wannabe Odysseus who's swum ashore. And what sort of hero is he? He couldn't put his postcards for her into the mail, let alone into bottles to cast overboard, but at least he bought them, found at all his ports of call, New Foundland, Santiago, San Diego . . . Who can forget those scenes of her checking her mail, collecting only bills and catalogs.

She Did Not Consult Eliot on the Naming of Cats

She named her cat Bryan Williams because she was tired of Fluffies and Dusties and Rovers, though she admitted that Rover was a much better name for a cat than a dog. An outdoor cat. She didn't name the cat Brian Wilson or Brian Jones—she wasn't of the sixties music generation. She wanted me to write the cat's story, but what was in the life of Bryan? Kittenhood, getting fixed, catnip, mouse, mouse, sparrow, mouse. She didn't name it Anderson Cooper or Soledad O'Brien. Bryan Williams—the cat was a tiger, well groomed, straight forward, the kind of cat you could trust not to swipe at you when you brush it. It was a news anchor kind of cat. She liked the news with Brian Williams. I could live with a woman like her, live with a cat like that. She watches the news. She scratches the kitty beneath the chin. Brian Williams gives a view of the day while Bryan Williams mews.

Girl Before a Mirror

—Pablo Picasso

I can see her and see her again, and of course, she might see me, too, there in the upper corner, watching her freshly showered, unselfconscious, naked and gorgeous. The girl in the reflection isn't her and is her both—a lefty reaching out to touch her right hand as she wipes condensation from the glass. All night she slept while the two-faced moon spied through the window. I want to put my hand on her belly, feel her skin powdery beneath my palm, but let's face it, should I approach, another me will show up before her, that seducer, unbidden. No doubt he loves her as well, or at least he'd say so. She must know better than to trust such a man, what with my arm encroaching her waist, the words I whisper into her dyed hair.

Last Saturday

I'd been invited to visit a woman who lived beneath a bridge in Central Park and whose eyes were two different types of clouds—the left one stratus, the right cirrus. It was easy to forecast her mood by how she gazed at me. She made tea on a trash can fire, spoke of NYU and the NYPD, her MBA and the MTA. She gave up a 401K and a personal trainer to be this close to penguins and to the man who makes bubbles that move above sidewalks like Chinese dragons. She was born in the year of the tiger. I in the month of the lion. Dog walkers gripped their leashes more tightly when they heard our laughter clamoring from below, rising to rattle the new leaves on the sycamores. Those dogs pulled harder toward home.

Later in the Planetarium I'll study photographs of earth taken from space and be amazed by how much it resembles her left eye and by how tiny the world must look from that distance.

Pocket Watch

Its is the face I hate looking at, the mirror in which I constantly appear older in increments, more cynical, more sallow. Yet, is there anything about this now I'd hold eternal?

Perfect anthology of 43,200 lyric moments, each one of them oscillating between breathtaking and forgettable, between mendacious and mundane, I open its cover, close it again return to the narrative of today in our year of the Lord.

At night, the rings on its jeweled fingers glow green to steer me toward some untoward destination,

and still not a compass, for there's no true north, not even at midnight, not even at noon, not even in the hour in between, dawn lighting the east. Each morning I tighten the spring the way I was taught, so taut it can catapult the sun across the sky.

Landmine

They only exist in motion pictures, those mines that explode only when someone steps off them. It's a plot device. In this way then is ours a Hollywood romance: to fall for her—how surprising, how barely buried but unforeseen was it. Such is chance. There are so many spring wires. I can stand here all day till I can't stand anymore. As long as I stay still, I'll be fine. I don't dare sigh, for the blast would tear the screen, tear up the audience in the theater rooting for the good soldier. I don't dare risk the detonation of this paradise, for we both know what devastation follows the kaboom.

CLOUDBURST

It's raining cats and frogs. It's raining bats and dogs. It's raining Laurel and Hardy, Bogey and Bacall, plain and peanut. It's raining peanut butter and jelly smeared on the window so neither of us can see outside. It's raining, it's pouring and the old man comes rolling home bedraggled, puddle weary, mud ugly. Thunder like the engine of the universe trying to turn over, the carburetor flooded. It's raining. It's raining nickels and dimes. It's raining pins and needles. We knuckle down: no one should go out on a night like tonight, Mother might say. Noah knew a downpour like this. It's raining old and new testament. I have a large umbrella. You have your new rubber boots. The wind is screaming somebody's name like a mother calling long after curfew.

Wingtips

In the back of the closet where I keep the things I've given up: the smoking jacket, the cardigan, the bolo tie with its black string and its silver and turquoise clasp, the cowboy boots I bought at the spur of the moment, among those costumes and props of another life, there where I'd hidden the could-have-been-mes, the better-mes, and worse-mes, too, I find my wingtips—two-tone and dusty—and lift them each for inspection. *They'd look good on you*, you insist, and you might be right, if only I knew what I'd done with the rest of my wings.

Toe Nail

It cracks like a mirror, comes with its size seven years bad luck. It breaks and splinters. There's the fear of it becoming ingrown, of it just being gone (the way my mother's is just gone, and how, in her vanity, she paints the skin where it once was red). But it remains, split like a windscreen hit by gravel. I'm no podiatrist. No pedicurist. I'm not pedantic in the least. Give me a foot, and I might take a yard, of course—that's the type of guy I can be.

Yet the nail dangles like a limp rag, the cleaning crew having called it a day. It won't slough off, what with the bandages and super glue. But the whole toe, the bigness of it? You never know when it might vanish, taking the nail with it. That's liable to be a bigger problem, a more pronounced limp.

A Short Lesson in Human Anatomy

The child holds a white balloon like a skull on a string. Her neighbor, a few years older and already a fan of dragons, owns a ceramic skull with a candle melting along its dome, a Niagara of red wax, of black wax. He chants spells at midnight, savoring the incantations, but nothing changes.

The average weight of the human head is eight to twelve pounds; of the skull alone, one quarter that. I like to think of your head on my chest, the indentation that weight makes in the flesh. Nothing ever changes. An average man, my heart weighs about twelve ounces. Under that pressure, it beats in excitement, beats in distress.

TARANTULA

I keep its shed exoskeleton the way I've kept my worn leather jacket, stiffened by absence. Having been both, it knows the exact meanings of hunter, of prey. How punk rock its binary spiny hairs; how not, my meager nostalgia. I know the tarantula doesn't mourn its molted skin, just as I know the woman I yearn for is not in my past.

I used to hold it in my palm for it was the size of my palm. I'd pet it with one finger, though sometimes it would rise on its hind legs and hiss. When it bit me, I sucked the venom from the wound though I knew it couldn't kill me, and knew, too, the pleasure of that burn. Sometimes, I'll say it loved me, but truly I know otherwise.

MACKEREL AND BOTTLE

—William Scott

Not the holy mackerel of the exclamation, nor the ones caught and served by the disciples to feed five thousand. Nope. Only ordinary mackerel: two of them for the two of us waiting for the frying pan.

The wine, too, from the liquor store's middle shelf for our middle class aspirations: a middling white, opened to breathe.

But there's only one glass set out, for I remembered you'd gone. Thus, I've invited the overcast skies inside. Don't be condescending: I haven't been crying. That's only condensation moist on my cheek.

Despite my prayers of intercession, my supplications for your safe return, I don't say grace. Instead, I cook the fish whole, plate them that way, so their eyes gaze at me while I dine, desperate as I am for company.

Thinking of You

I like to think of you since I think.
                    –Jaime Sabines

I like to think of you in the shower, not because I like to imagine your body naked, sheened with water (though I do), but because of how you sing in the spray songs I can't decipher.

I like to think of you at the table at work while I am at the table at work, our table like an unscrolled map of a continent I would cross on horseback if I must. Every day I consult the almanac of your name.

I like to think of you in the waning minutes of light before full dark in the country where full dark still exists and how you become in that moment dusky, mysterious. Your earrings, the night's first stars.

I like to think of you writing this postcard in invisible ink, the one I turn over in my hands with my morning coffee, my morning scratch of the cat's head.

I like to think of you because I am when I think and I am more-than when I think of you. Now is not the time for a lesson on less-than thoughts.

Of course, you've heard such things before—guys almost like me are lined up in soup lines. They hunger. They thirst. I like to think of you so I can continue to go without.

GRATITUDE:

I live in a community of fine writers and artists and loved ones who all contribute to my work and deserve thanks.

First to my students, who remind me that writing is to be in awe of language and to be open to surprise, and to Frostburg State University and Carlow University's MFA Program for their continued belief in my work and my teaching. To Kim Davis and Madville Publishing for their belief in these prose poems and for their fine detail and attention to making this book happen. To Rick Campbell and Bob Kunzinger, who introduced me to Madville, and to Janet Lowery for her kind and gracious support of this manuscript, and to Laura McCullough for the generous blurb.

Thanks and more thanks to Elena Feliciano whose paintings I admire and who let me use her artwork again for the cover of this book. She's the real deal.

A special shout out to my writer friends, George Guida, Stephen Dunn, Jan Beatty, Joe Fasano, Jennifer Browne, Jack DuBose, Joy Gaines Friedler, Marty Williams, Michael Waters, Tim Seibles, Lynn McGee, and Madeleine Barnes. They inspire me. They support me. They kick my ass to be a better writer and better person. To Fred Powell and Main Street Books (Frostburg, MD). To Alex LaFemina, who daily reminds me of the pleasures of the surreal and the whimsical, of the campy and the sublime. To my mother, Toni, the best poetry mom in the States. To Mercedes Hettich, both for the photograph and the love.

And, of course, to my readers. That you have chosen this book is a gift to me.

I offer apologies to anyone I might have accidentally left out.

ABOUT THE AUTHOR

Gerry LaFemina's latest books are the poetry collection *The Story of Ash* (Anhinga, 2018) and a new chapbook, *Points South* (Hysterical Books, 2019). His previous books include a novel, a collection of short stories, and numerous award-winning collections of poetry, including *The Parakeets of Brooklyn*, *Notes for the Novice Ventriloquist* (prose poems), *Vanishing Horizon*, and *Little Heretic*. His essays on poets and prosody, *Palpable Magic*, came out on Stephen F Austin University Press and his textbook, *Composing Poetry: A Guide to Writing Poems and Thinking Lyrically* was released by Kendall Hunt. The former director of the Frostburg Center for Literary Arts and a current Fulbright Specialist, he teaches at Frostburg State University and serves as a Mentor in the MFA Program at Carlow University.

www.ingramcontent.com/pod-product-compliance
Lightning Source LLC
Chambersburg PA
CBHW042047090426
42733CB00039B/2659